MINIATURE HORSES

WEIRD PETS

Lynn M. Stone

Rourke Publishing LLC
Vero Beach, Florida 32964

www.rourkepublishing.com

PHOTO CREDITS:
© Norvia Behling: Pages 8, 12
© Daniel Johnson: Page 10; © Lynn M. Stone: Cover, Pages 4, 7, 13, 15, 17, 18, 21

EDITORIAL SERVICES:
Pamela Schroeder

Library of Congress Cataloging-in-Publication Data

Stone, Lynn M.
    Miniature horses/ Lynn M. Stone
        p. cm.— (Weird pets)
    ISBN 1-58952-039-4
    1. Miniature horses—Juvenile literature. [1. Miniature horses. 2. Horses. 3. Pets.] I. Title

SF293.M56 S76 2001
636.1'09—dc21   2001017053

Printed in the USA

TABLE OF CONTENTS

MINIATURE HORSES

Miniature, or mini, horses gallop, whinny, and nibble on each others' necks. They munch hay and crunch sugar cubes. They act like any other horse. They have long, flowing **manes** and tails. They have thin legs and long heads. They even look like other horses—except for size.

A beautiful miniature horse stallion races across his paddock.

Miniatures are little horses, just as bantams are little chickens. The American Miniature Horse Association (AMHA) says a miniature horse cannot stand taller than 34 inches (87 centimeters) from the ground to the bottom of its mane. A mini horse and a St. Bernard dog stand about eye-to-eye.

Miniature horses are not new. People have been raising small horses for at least 400 years. Most of the North American minis came from **breeds** such as Morgans, Hackneys, Arabs, and Shetlands.

Miniature horses are found in Canada and in all 50 United States.

MINIATURE HORSES: PET FRIENDLY?

Mini horses are too small to ride or do work. So why would anyone want a horse that can't be ridden or worked?

Many people love horses. But those people don't all ride horses, nor do they all want to ride. A mini horse may be perfect for these people.

Children are safer around miniature horses than full-size horses.

Not everyone who would like a horse has the space to keep it. After all, most horses weigh 1,000 pounds (450 kilograms) or even more. A mini horse needs less room than a big horse—and it eats less food!

Mini horses can be trained to pull small carts.

Children can take an active part in raising and caring for miniature horses.

Horses are herd animals and feel safe with each other.

If you can't ride a miniature horse, what can you do with it? Mini horse owners might say, what can you do with a rabbit, canary, or cockatoo? Many miniature horse owners just like having horses around. Their little horses are family pets.

Some mini horse owners train their animals to pull carts, jump, or race around **obstacles**. Many owners bring their horses to AMHA shows to compete against other minis.

This handsome miniature stallion is one of his breeder's best horses.

Away from cities, a few mini horses are being used as guides for people who can't see. These horses are trained by the Guide Horse Foundation.

Mini horses are good pets for people with the time to care for them. They are curious and gentle, and they like human attention. They are safer around children than full-size horses.

A mini horse breeder combs a young horse, called a foal.

CARING FOR MINIATURE HORSES

Like cats and dogs, horses are **domestic**, or tame, animals. They need people to give them food, water, shelter, health care, and attention.

Miniature horses should have barns or sheds for shelter. They also need a pasture or **paddock**. There they can exercise, graze, and visit with each other. Horses are herd animals and like to be with each other.

Owners make sure their horses have plenty of water and a healthy diet. Mini horses mostly eat dry food pellets.

Owners help keep their horses' coats, or hair, clean and shiny by **grooming** them. They use special brushes and combs.

Veterinarians, or animal doctors, treat mini horses for any health problems. Vets also give shots to horses to keep them from getting sick.

Hoping for a treat, a mini horse stallion trots along with its keeper.

FINDING A MINIATURE HORSE

Do you think you want a miniature horse? Before buying one, you need to do some homework. For example, is it a good idea to buy a **foal**, or baby horse? Would it be better to buy an older, trained horse?

Breeders raise mini horses, foals and adults. Find at least one breeder to talk to. You can find breeders in horse magazines or on-line through the AMHA. Ask questions! Look for an alert, friendly horse with a shiny coat.

GLOSSARY

breed (BREED) — within a certain group of domestic animals, such as horses, one separate group with its own traits, such as a *Morgan* horse

breeder (BREED er) — a person who raises a kind of animal to sell to other people

domestic (deh MES tik) — refers to a type of animal that has been kept by people and tamed for many years, perhaps thousands

foal (FOHL) — a baby horse

grooming (GROOM ing) — making an animal look neat by combing or brushing

mane (MAYN) — the long hair on a horse's forehead and neck

obstacle (AHB steh kel) — anything that stands in the way, such as a hurdle

paddock (PAD ek) — an outdoor pen, especially for horses

veterinarian (vet er eh NAYR ee en) — an animal doctor

INDEX

Further Reading

Stone, Lynn M. *Read All About Horses*. Rourke Publishing, 1998
Wilcox, Charlotte. *Miniature Horses*. Children's Press, 1997

Websites To Visit

•www.amha.com   •www.ansi.okstate.edu/breeds/horses/miniature

About The Author

Lynn Stone is the author of over 400 children's books. He is a talented natural history photographer as well. Lynn, a former teacher, travels worldwide to photograph wildlife in their natural habitat.